House Beautiful
SMALL SPACE
DECORATING WORKSHOP

House Beautiful
SMALL SPACE
DECORATING WORKSHOP

TESSA EVELEGH

Hearst Books

A Division of Sterling Publishing Co., Inc.

New York

Created, edited, and designed by Duncan Baird Publishers Ltd., Castle House, 75–76 Wells Street, London W1T 3QH

Managing editor: Emma Callery
Designer: Alison Shackleton

Photographs: see credits on page 158. The publisher has made every effort to properly credit the photographers whose work appears in this book. Please let us know if an error has been made, and we will make any necessary changes in subsequent printings.

Library of Congress Cataloging-in-Publication Data
House Beautiful small space decorating workshop / [from the editors of House Beautiful].
    p. cm.
Includes index.
ISBN 1-58816-495-0
    1. Small rooms--Decoration. 2. Interior decoration.
I. Title: Small space decorating workshop.
NK2117.S59H68 2005
747'.1--dc22

2005046037

1 2 3 4 5 6 7 8 9 10

Published by Hearst Books
A Division of Sterling Publishing Co., Inc.
387 Park Avenue South, New York, NY 10016

House Beautiful is a trademark of
Hearst Communications, Inc.

www.housebeautiful.com

For information about custom editions, special sales, premium and corporate purchases, please contact Sterling Special Sales Department at 800-805-5489 or specialsales@sterlingpub.com.

Distributed in Canada by Sterling Publishing
c/o Canadian Manda Group, 165 Dufferin Street
Toronto, Ontario, Canada M6K 3H6

Distributed in Australia by Capricorn Link
(Australia) Pty. Ltd., P. O. Box 704, Windsor,
NSW 2756 Australia

Manufactured in China.
ISBN 1–58816-495-0

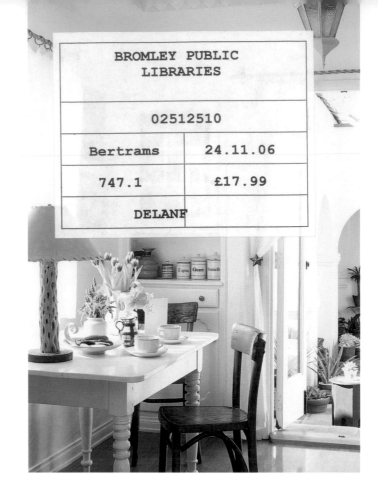

CONTENTS

Foreword 6

FIRST THINGS FIRST 9
Finding extra space 10
The great divide 14
From awkward to useful 18
Multifunctional space 20
Storage 24

THE CREATIVE APPROACH 35
A fresh approach 36
Less is more 38
Small room, big furniture 40
Color 42
Pattern & texture 44
Window treatments 46
Using mirrors 48
Flexible furniture 50
Occasional furniture 52
Everyday display 54

ROOM BY ROOM 57
Living 61
Cooking 73
Eating 85
Sleeping 97
Bathing 109
Working 121
Connecting spaces 131

MEETING THE CHALLENGE 141
Making it work 142
Lofts 144
Attic rooms 146
Curved walls 148
Alcoves 150
Awkward floor plans 152
Too many windows 154
One-room living 156

Photography credits 158
Index 158

FOREWORD

How do you make the best of small space living? This is a question I am often asked by *House Beautiful* readers. How do you fit everything in, they ask? Where do you stow the essentials of life? How do you bring a sleek modern look to a room of limited proportions? How do you find space to entertain friends when your home is bursting at the seams? These questions are all addressed in the pages of this book.

Although there are no hard and fast rules to small space living, there are pointers that can help you to think through your home, your lifestyle, and what would work best for you and your family. Architects and interior designers always start by assessing the space. They look for "dead" alcoves, niches, corridors, or corners which can be brought efficiently into play. They analyze furniture arrangements to check whether they make the best use of the space. They look at storage to check that it is being used to its fullest advantage, or if there are any spare corners where new shelves or cupboards can be added. With careful planning and a few adaptations, it's amazing what extra useful space can be squeezed from your home, even without consulting a builder.

Even if the space has been used efficiently, it can still look small or cramped, depending on how it has been decorated and furnished. Pastel or lively color choices and reflective surfaces, such as mirrors, which maximize the natural daylight, can quickly transform a gloomy room into one with a much brighter, more welcoming ambience. Window treatments, too, can enhance the natural light. Instead of hanging elaborate drapes, which tend to encroach on the windowpanes and obliterate the light, choose simpler solutions, such as shades or uncomplicated panels. Clever furniture choices can also help to visually open up small rooms, creating a greater feeling of space. This book shows you how to embrace what traditional

rules tell us to avoid. For example, it demonstrates the effect of choosing large pieces of furniture and making them work in small rooms.

To complement the basic principles of small space furnishing, the "Room by Room" chapter looks at how they can be applied in a practical way to each situation.

Finally, I make no apologies for tackling storage issues at every opportunity. Efficient living in any size home depends on excellent storage. In small spaces it becomes paramount if you don't want to be overwhelmed by the paraphernalia of everyday living. Dip into the chapters and you'll discover how to think through your storage needs, find space for storage—even in limited rooms—and how to organize the interiors of closets for the most efficient ways to keep your belongings.

If you plan to be a little more ambitious about your small space living and take on some professional advice, you'll find food for thought right here. There are ideas for begging, borrowing, and stealing space from one area to give to another that make your home work better for you. There are suggestions on how to look upward to make use of loft space, and there's plenty to think about when it comes to kitchens. All this is food for thought, so you can work out what best suits your lifestyle and help you put together your ideas for a professional designer or builder.

But whatever your situation, if you live in a home with small, or even awkward rooms, I hope you'll find *Small Space Decorating Workshop* a useful companion. It's packed with bite-size information designed to help you make the very best of small space living.

MARK MAYFIELD
Editor in Chief, *House Beautiful*

FIRST
THINGS
FIRST

FINDING EXTRA SPACE

Where space is at a premium, every square inch counts, and the way in which it is organized can make a huge difference in the usefulness of the rooms in your home. Finding extra space falls into two overall categories: The first and easiest solution is to make every part of every room work hard, with efficient use of furniture and storage. If that is still unlikely to solve your space problems, you can always look at remodeling the interior. This won't necessarily come cheap, but it is usually well worth the cost and effort, as it is often less expensive and disruptive than moving. Also, even the most modest remodeling of your home provides an opportunity to really think through your lifestyle and decide what is truly essential and what is dispensible.

▲ Hardworking hall

Furnish the hall with a sofa and table, and award yourself an extra seating area. Allow at least 30 inches for passing between the front edge of the sofa and opposite wall.

▶ Go through the roof

When the house seems to be bursting at the seams, look to the roof space. An extra sitting room in a loft has been coaxed from this one.

Inspired solutions

◆ **Seek out the slimmest pieces of furniture** that can fit into narrow spaces, providing both storage surfaces for accessories and a place to "park" belongings on the move, such as letters, parcels, keys, and gloves.

◆ **Find flexible furniture** that can be folded, stacked, and stowed away when not needed, but brought into useful service wherever and whenever it's needed.

◆ **Make corners work** by building in seating, thereby using every spare inch.

◆ **Choose furniture** that relates to the space. Better to have one large four-seater sofa that spans the length of a wall than a three-seater, which leaves dead space at either end.

◆ **Provide plenty of storage,** even if by doing so, you sacrifice an inch or two of living space. If you can't put everything away, the usable space you do have will soon become cluttered.

◆ **Use alcoves and niches** for seating, thereby extending the main living space.

◆ **Think vertically.** Closets and shelving need not encroach much on the floor space, but you can fit a lot of shelves up to the ceiling, providing a surprising amount of storage. Don't forget about small, neglected spaces, such as those above a door.

◆ **Take a corner** and make it work by furnishing it with a small table or desk, for example. You'll be surprised how many landings, halls, and family rooms have "dead" space that could accommodate a mini-office.

◆ **Look under the stairs.** The space could possibly be converted into a powder room or a desk space.

◆ **Steal some space** from the landing to make capacious cupboards and free up the bedrooms.

◆ **Move partition walls,** taking space from a bedroom to make a half bath. Consult a building professional to check that the walls are not load-bearing, which must never be moved.

◆ **Look to the ceiling space** and create a loft.

◆ **Go for a loft** to squeeze in an extra room at mezzanine level. This only works if you have sufficient ceiling height in the first place.

▲ Steal a corner

The corner of this bedroom has been put to good use as an office. Shelves squeezed between the wall and post provide ample book storage, while a simple two-piece desk offers both laptop and layout space.

▶ Window seating

Build seats into window bays or alcoves, and you'll gain extra seating that does not encroach on the main living area. The table placed near this window seat is joined by two occasional chairs to gain a great dining area.

THE GREAT DIVIDE

When living accommodation is limited, consider opening up your space. Open plan living has become increasingly popular because it offers very effective use of space and shared light. Although open plan is often associated with large spaces, it can work just as effectively in smaller areas, and the principles remain the same whatever the scale. Part of the success lies in how you "zone" the space, drawing boundaries for each area.

There are basically three ways to do this: You can use floor finishes; install screens or sliding doors; or carefully position the furniture.

Floor finishes signal different functions around the home. For example, you may use a resilient stone or slate in the cooking zone and warmer wood in the dining area. Even if the floor has already been laid, you can use the same principle by putting a rug in the seating

▲ Slide show
Sliding doors make ideal room dividers as they can either be left open or closed to create separate rooms. Made from translucent material, these allow light to filter through from one area to another, even when closed.

▶ Back-to-back
By backing the sitting area against the kitchen, this space is essentially two rooms. A wall between them would not only take up usable space, it would also diminish the considerable amount of shared light.

area, signaling comfort in direct contrast to the hard floor of a kitchen.

Sliding doors or floor-to-ceiling panels are a more obvious way of demarking different areas: by closing them, you can even create separate rooms. Screens are extremely useful dividing devices as they can be moved to create flexible areas—larger or smaller as required—or even put away if you need one large space, when

▶ **Island boundary**
The central island unit in this kitchen neatly divides the cooking from eating areas. The shape of the furniture sends out subliminal messages, too. The round dining table covered with a pretty printed cloth implies relaxation in contrast to the straight lines of the kitchen.

entertaining, for example. Open bookshelves are a clever way to create permanent screening as they provide a division, allow light to filter through from one area to another, and, even better, offer storage.

Open spaces can also be zoned with a clever arrangement of fixed and movable furniture. A kitchen island unit, for example, can form a boundary between cooking and eating areas, and the back of a sofa could be used to create a "wall" between sitting and dining.

▲ Multifunctional divisions

Floor-to-ceiling bookshelves divide the family room from the main sitting area. It's a clever idea because the room divider also serves as a capacious bookcase.

▶ Thrice as nice

This open plan kitchen and utility area have been cleverly designed to give ultimate flexibility with three types of divisions. The floor is hard-wearing slate in the utility area with hardwood flooring in the cooking zone. The central kitchen unit also marks the boundary. Finally, the pantry and utility are divided by a sliding door, which can be closed when entertaining.

FROM AWKWARD TO USEFUL

Useful space can be coaxed from even the most unlikely crannies, so don't write off those under-the-stairs, under-the-eaves, alcove, or corridor areas. Even rooms that have as little as a four-foot width of floorspace and enough headroom to stand up can be transformed into a room that makes a difference to the whole house. Areas with limited headroom can become useful if furniture or closets are positioned under the lower parts of the roof, leaving the maximum amount of space with full headroom.

Landing nooks and crannies can be transformed into closets that encompass serious storage, relieving other rooms of the burden. Areas little larger than closets themselves can become very effective shower stalls (see pages 118–119). Tiny strips of space can be transformed into small kitchens or offices (see pages 138–139). Some of these ideas can be realized with clever positioning of furniture. If you've decided to be more ambitious and remodel the interior, always get the advice of a building professional to ensure you don't put the house in danger of structural damage.

Inspired solutions

◆ **Install desk space and closets** in areas where the eaves are low, reserving the areas with headroom for circulation. You could be surprised how little circulation space you need for an effective office.
◆ **Run closets right across** awkward areas to create a sleeker look to a room, then fill them with useful shelving and drawers.

▶ **Lack of headroom**

This would have been a roomy bedroom, had it not been up in the roof space. But, rather than using just one end of the room (to the left of the photograph) for the bed, and "losing" those parts lacking in headroom under the eaves, seating has been positioned under the windows where you don't need the headroom.

▲ **Too narrow**

This space is so narrow there isn't even a wall long enough for a regular bath. The solution has been to install a hot tub, which is designed for sitting, rather than lying, and is shorter but deeper than a regular bath.

◀ Too thin

This tiny strip of space has been turned into a highly efficient galley kitchen. Plan for cupboards under the counter and add further ample storage on open shelves above, which keep the room looking light and airy.

With space only on the right-hand side of the window for open shelves, extra shelving has been located on the opposite wall to the left of the window, thereby keeping everything close to hand.

There is space only for one line of units in this extremely narrow strip of space.

This small space was in danger of being gloomy, so it has been painted white and fitted with white units to enhance the area as much as possible.

MULTIFUNCTIONAL SPACE

When space is short, make it work twice as hard. A kitchen table can become a dining table, homework table, sewing table, and even a desk if you're very organized. A sitting room can be transformed into a comfortable guest room, given a daybed, futon, or sofa bed. A hallway with space for a table can occasionally be dressed up as a dining area; if there's room for a sofa or couple of chairs, it can become a reception area. A dining room, which needs little furniture, can spend most of its time disguised as a playroom. When the table is pushed to one side, there'll be plenty of space for play, while providing the best surface for painting and craft work—but seek out a good quality plastic-coated cloth

▶ Studio glamor

This tiny room elegantly combines sleeping and relaxing. Under-the-bed drawers conveniently deal with storage, and with the addition of handsome black and white bolsters, the bed takes on a sofa-like personality. Even so, the generous drapes can be drawn across the bed, should guests arrive before you've had time to plump the pillows.

◀ Relaxed dining

Here's a pretty pastel room that spends most of its time as a sitting room. When guests are expected for dinner, a round occasional table is brought out, covered with a crisp white cloth and joined by chairs gathered from all around the apartment. The result is a delightful and inviting dining area.

to protect the table's surface. If the toys are stacked in boxes and kept in a closet, they can quickly be neatened and the table pulled into the dining position when guests are due. Given enough closets to store iron, ironing board, and laundry basket, a guest bedroom can become the ironing room between times, or an office with a sofa bed can be quickly transformed into a guest bedroom when the need arises.

Most of these ideas depend on two supporting "players": excellent storage (see pages 24–33) and flexible furniture (see pages 50–51). With planned storage, you can easily stow the paraphernalia associated with the various activities. Flexible furniture can either be transformed for alternative uses (by extending it or opening it out), or it can be on patient standby until needed. Look for furniture that can be folded down, folded up, stacked, stored, or hung up out of the way.

▲ Three times table
This table, positioned as it is between kitchen and living room, can take on many guises, ranging from kitchen to dining table. It's also a delightful place to tackle the household paperwork.

▶ Living and working
By containing a whole office in a pretty colored cabinet that teams with the upholstery, this living room has double the use.

STORAGE

Storage has to be a priority for all efficiently run homes. The Shaker ideal was "a place for everything and everything in its place." As the Shakers lived communally, everyone needed to be able to put everything away in the right place, and to find quickly what he needed when he needed it. To address this, they built efficient wall-to-wall storage units consisting of both drawers and cupboards, providing plenty of space for all their belongings. The same principles apply to any contemporary family home.

If you don't have the storage space to put everything away, it's both difficult to tidy up and difficult to find anything. Even worse for the main tidier-upper of the home, it's almost impossible to delegate much of the tidying. Small space living means that efficient storage becomes even more important, because just a few things out of place create a muddle. Even if space is seriously limited, it really is worth sacrificing a little to efficient storage for the sake of organized living. The good news about awkward spaces is that they often incorporate odd alcoves and niches that are good for very little in terms of living space; but built-in shelves or closets and what was dead space can become very useful.

▶▲ Cupboard love
Cupboards, as well as shelves, can be fitted into alcoves. Here, the lower ones have solid doors, while the glass-fronted upper ones can be used to display attractive china.

▶ Upper echelons
Dead space can be found in all sorts of places. Here, even short lengths of wall on either side of the window and a narrow strip above it add up to generous book shelving.

▶▶ Efficient alcoves
Building bookshelves into alcoves is a favorite trick that transforms dead space into efficient storage. Built-in shelves can also be tailor-made to fit under sloping eaves.

STORAGE: BUILT-IN

One of the best uses of awkward spaces is to transform them into built-in closets. This not only gives you efficient storage, but it can also improve the proportions of the room. For example, a closet may span a wall, taking in alcoves, niches, and sloping ceilings, squaring off the room in the process. Or you may have an uncomfortably long, thin room. In this instance, by running a closet the full length of one of the short walls, you can create versatile storage space and, at the same time,

transform the room to a much more comfortable shape. If you are in the privileged position of having closets custom-built, start by assessing the dimensions of the items you want to store. This will not only help you to work out the overall amount of storage space you need, but it will also encourage you to consider just how you want to divide the closets for maximum efficiency (see "Bedroom Storage," pages 102–103, and "Office Storage," pages 128–129).

▶ Divide and rule

Built-in or freestanding, it's the internal organization that makes closets efficient. This one has special shoe storage in the doors, so every pair can be seen at a glance. One side of the closet has two hanging rails to accommodate plenty of short garments, and one high hanging rail for longer clothing.

▶▶ Modular success

Designed on a modular system, this built-in unit incorporates drawers, cupboards, file holders, and cubbyholes. A system such as this can be put together to suit individual needs. Here, the space for four units has been combined to accommodate the television.

STORAGE: SHELVING

For efficient bookshelves, display, or general kitchen shelves, all you need is a depth of just ten inches. However, depending on what you plan to store, even six inches can provide useful storage for food cans, cooking ingredients, and spice jars.

Open shelving can be attached directly to the wall using uprights and brackets or brackets on their own.

They can be custom-made as a built-in unit, or bought as freestanding units. If you are buying freestanding, aim to fill the available wall space for most efficient storage. Some freestanding shelves come in modular form and can be put together to suit the space. It's even possible to build them in step form to fit under sloping ceilings or staircases.

▲ Easy reach
Open shelves work well in small kitchens as you can make an attractive display of everyday casseroles, bowls, china, and glass, while having everything in sight and within easy reach. The whole ensemble also brings a light and airy look to even the most awkward of kitchens.

▲ Built-in style
This custom-made bookshelf has been designed to fit between the fireplace and its adjoining wall, complete with molding, to suit the style of the room.

▶ Movable feast
This simple, ready-made shelving unit not only provides plenty of storage space, but can be moved around on its wheels. In this situation it doubles up as a room divider, but it would look equally good against a wall.

STORAGE: FREESTANDING

There's a long tradition for freestanding storage furniture such as cupboards, chests of drawers, and sideboards. Antique pieces still make a pretty addition to any interior while offering very useful storage space. There are plenty of modern counterparts and new pieces have been added to their numbers to deal with the storage of modern entertainment equipment, such as televisions, sound systems, video recorders, and DVD players, as well as the associated media of CDs, DVDs, and videos. Whether you're buying old or new, carefully measure the available space, including the ceiling height, and mark it on a sketch before setting out. Take it and the measuring tape with you to the shops to ensure the piece will fit into the allocated area.

▲ All change
A pretty painted wooden wardrobe, picked up from a secondhand shop, introduces color to this simple bedroom. The advantage of this style of furniture is that it can be repainted to suit any changes to the décor.

▲▲ Show off
Pretty linens deserve to be shown off in a glass-front cabinet, introducing color to the room.

▲ Antique beauty
An antique polished mahogany chest of drawers, like this exquisite bow-fronted version, is a beautiful focal point in a bedroom.

◄ On the side
An antique sideboard makes the perfect piece of dining room furniture, combining drawers for the storage of cutlery, place mats, and candles.

STORAGE: DETAILS

Storage is as much about the way in which you organize your belongings on the shelves and in the closets as it is about the fittings themselves. Even capacious cupboards are far from efficient if everything they hold is a disorganized mess. Items on shelves need to relate to the size of the shelves: spice jars on small shelves; serving dishes on large. Another solution is to arrange smaller items in containers on the shelves: a basket each for socks, handkerchiefs, and ties can fit together happily on a single closet shelf in the bedroom; boxes in the bathroom cabinet can each contain cosmetics, medicines, shampoos, and suntan protection. In children's rooms, toys can be arranged in plastic bins by type: one for cars, another for farmyard animals, a third for fashion dolls, and a fourth for their clothes. Sorting them like this can become the first lessons for children in organization and cleaning up, because putting everything away becomes a game.

▲ Hung up

Hooks on the back of the door are the simplest of storage solutions. These are smocks, but they could just as well be bathrobes—hang one hook on the back of the bathroom door for each member of the family.

▲ Tidy display

Foot-size shelving is the perfect storage for shoes. In these vertical ranks, each pair is clearly visible; and all together, they combine to make a striking display in this cheerful, informal bedroom.

◀ Overlapping ranks

Even if you have only the narrowest space for shelves, there's room for effective storage. This plate rack provides a home for everyday dinnerware when lined up, face forward. Efficient and always at hand, this represents an excellent use of space.

◀ Everything in its place

Storage is at its most efficient when the items to be used are near at hand. Here, cooking utensils hang above the stove, just where they're needed. Pots and pans dangle from an overhead rack, easily within reach of the cooking area. Narrow shelves in front of the window are perfect for storing jars of cooking ingredients. It's a kitchen with everything on display, all items being organized in size-related storage.

THE
CREATIVE
APPROACH

A FRESH APPROACH

Take a new look at the small rooms in your home and you might be surprised what you can do to make them feel lighter, more airy, and less cramped without even consulting a builder. What might at first glance seem awkward either due to lack of space or because windows, doors, and alcoves are inconveniently positioned, can take on a whole new persona with a coat of paint, re-arrangement of the furniture, or even investment in a new table, sofa, or piece of storage.

Color can offer the quickest transformation. Paler shades give a feeling of space, so paint over deep tones and move out dark, overbearing pieces of furniture (or give them a coat of paint, too), and the room will immediately feel larger. Next, encourage as much light into the room as possible by keeping window treatments simple and letting in light from other rooms, for example, by replacing door panels with glass. You can also use mirrors to reflect, and therefore magnify, the available light.

Another way to make small rooms really work for you is to look at your furniture—do those two small sofas you brought with you from a previous home truly work here? Or would you be able to accommodate more people more comfortably on one huge sofa that better suits the dimensions of the room?

Finally, rethink your clutter, which has a habit of diminishing the feeling of space. Plan to keep just a few gorgeous pieces, which will then create a much more restful interior. Store unattractive essentials in efficient storage systems, saving display areas for the more visual with favorite, smaller pieces grouped for impact.

▶ On reflection
Mirrors not only magnify the available light, but when fitted wall to wall, as here, they reflect the whole room, making it appear double its natural size.

▲ Flexible furnishing
This white-painted folding table is a perfect choice for any room of limited proportions. Light-reflective for a feeling of airiness, it is also highly flexible—a valuable consideration for small space furnishing. Fully open, it offers plenty of dining space; folded down to its smallest, it can become a neat console, allowing generous circulation space for entertaining in numbers.

▶ The big idea
Large-scale seating can be the unexpected solution for small room furnishing. Here, the sofa and side chairs fit snugly into a tiny space, but with the addition of a square table, they make for sophisticated dining.

LESS IS MORE

Clutter tends to visually accentuate the potentially cramped look of small spaces, so aim to ban as much as you can. Limit furniture to the bare minimum, with pieces chosen carefully for their usefulness, and when it comes to decorative items, use a few, larger decorative pieces rather than lots of little ones. From a practical viewpoint, of course, the paraphernalia of life consists of clutter, so aim to organize this decoratively or hide it, where you can, behind the doors of efficient closets. A bank of shelves or closets along one wall can accommodate an astonishing number of possessions, especially if they're well planned to suit their use.

Inspired solutions

◆ **Think minimal:** choose only really useful pieces of furniture and refuse to be distracted by anything you don't really need. One or two larger pieces that fit the space are invariably more useful than lots of little ones (see also page 40).

◆ **Work out your storage needs** and incorporate built-in storage designed to fit. For example, shelves for books need to be deeper and spaced further apart than those used for CDs; clothes hanging space needs to be slightly deeper than a hanger (see also page 26).

◆ **Run storage all along one wall if possible.** The closets will only steal a few inches from the room dimension, while offering generous amounts of clutter-concealing storage.

▲ **Bathing beauty**
A Victorian bathtub is all that is needed in this tiny attic bathroom. Positioned centrally, it turns a cramped space into one that feels well proportioned, light, and airy.

▶ **Stealthy storage**
This built-in storage unit running the length of one wall hardly makes any difference to the proportions of the room, yet gives a home to essential but potentially cluttering bits and pieces. The shelves have been designed to the dimensions of the books, which means they remain looking neat and orderly, while the drawers and cupboards below conceal a jumble of CDs and DVDs.

Simple cream shades keep the windows clutter-free, continuing the sleek theme.

The only essential piece of furniture in a bedroom is the bed, so here it is allowed to dominate the room, offering visual simplicity.

▼ **Peaceful sleep**

Light, airy, and clutter-free, this minimal bedroom promises easy relaxation due to lack of busyness in the interior design.

Small wooden bedside tables on either side of the bed visually recede, contributing to the minimal look.

An end-of-bed trunk is upholstered to match the bed. In this way, they visually become one item to continue the uncluttered look.

The tall, imposing stove is white-enameled, adding a decorative touch without dominating this elegantly simple room.

SMALL ROOM, BIG FURNITURE

If your small room has to work hard accommodating plenty of people on a daily basis, try avoiding the obvious. Instead of presuming small rooms have to be furnished with dainty furniture, aim to fill the room with a few large pieces that provide plenty of seats. The trick is to use every inch of space and make any "dead" corners work hard. Rooms designed for relaxation, such as living rooms, dining rooms, and bedrooms, need remarkably little circulation space as generally, once in the room, the aim is to sit down or lie down. Bearing this in mind, you can furnish "relaxation" rooms with large pieces that take up much of the space, which would not only offer plenty of seating, but also result in a well-organized, uncluttered look.

Inspired solutions

◆ **Careful measurement is the key to success**, so take a measured plan to the furniture store with you. Even once you have chosen the furniture, it would be advisable to mark out the dimensions in the room to check the fit before buying.

◆ **Look at the proportions of your room** and furnish it with pieces that reflect its size. Either use furniture that fills in "dead" space, or use central pieces that echo the shape of the room. For example, in a long thin space, use a narrow refectory or oval table, while square areas can be filled with square or round tables.

▶ **Intimate dining**

A narrow dining room need not mean a limited guest list. The best possible use of the space has been achieved here by choosing a table that reflects the proportions of the room. There's generous seating for eight and little wasted circulation space. When planning, allow a minimum of three feet of pullback space for chairs, depending on their design (see also page 88).

▶ **Fully fitted**

Corner sofas are an ideal way to make space work. Tucking into a corner that might otherwise be unused, this one offers ample seating in a small space, while also being sleek and simple in style.

An upholstered ottoman is flexible indeed. Topped by a tray, it can become a coffee table; with the tray removed, it offers seating for another two or even three people.

A wall-mounted lamp brings reading light to the corner where it's needed without sacrificing seating space to a side table or standard lamp.

The round ottoman tucks in close to the sofa. Its curved dimensions mean that circulation is easier than with an equivalent square stool or table.

Corner sofas are often supplied in modular form to allow a snug fit. This one comes in straight runs of two, three, or even four seats with a left or right end arm plus a separate corner piece.

COLOR

The hues we live with not only affect our mood, they also affect our perception of space. When decorating small spaces, the challenge is to avoid making them feel too cramped or overbearing. Colors that look good in other rooms may not necessarily work where space and light are limited. Strong colors that look good in a large space may be too dominating in a small one; neutrals, such as pebble tones, may look elegant in a generously proportioned room but appear prison-like or dismal in a more meager space.

As with any room, it's important to paint samples of your chosen color onto the walls so you can assess how it is affected by the light at different times of the day. Bearing in mind that paler tones tend to visually enlarge spaces and darker ones draw them in, aim to use color to enhance awkward spaces.

Inspired solutions

◆ Visually widen narrow rooms by using paler tones on the longer walls and deeper shades on the shorter ones, thereby drawing them in.

◆ "Raise" low ceilings by painting them paler than the rest of the room. You can also "lower" ceilings that appear too high by painting them a shade or two darker than the walls.

◆ Make a feature of alcoves and interesting niches by making them stand out with accent colors.

◆ Open up small rooms by decorating them with pale shades. If you love color, introduce this with furniture and accessories.

◆ Keep small rooms sleek by avoiding excessive detail. For example, paint moldings, picture rails, and chair rails to match the adjacent walls and create large blocks of color. The architectural detail will still be clearly thrown into relief, retaining the character of the room.

The striped pillows echo the accent colors in the rug.

Deep pink sofas bring a warm glow. The cream scatter pillows provide a color link with the walls.

A flamboyant pink potted plant extends the color vertically, thereby avoiding visually cutting the room in half horizontally.

Cream paint is used throughout the room to cover exposed brick walls, ceilings, shutters, and window jambs. This provides a neat canvas against which color can be introduced using furniture and accessories.

▲ Modern contrast

White walls throughout visually enlarge the limited space, but are given a sharp modern edge when teamed with a black-varnished floor. The glossy finish reflects, rather than absorbs, the light, contributing further to the feeling of light and space. Color is introduced with the bedclothes. Bright red, pink, and violet bring a vibrancy that is given a sophisticated edge with the use of gunmetal gray.

◀ Pretty in pink

Rosy hues create a warm, relaxed ambience in this intimate living room, which nevertheless looks surprisingly light and airy.

The chintz covering the footrest provides a satiny surface that reflects the light

The striped rug incorporates the cream of the walls and pinks of the furniture to link the design. Touches of green, purple, and yellow provide accent colors.

PATTERN & TEXTURE

Small and awkward spaces don't generally respond well to large or dominant designs: first, because they can overwhelm the room, and second, because there's little space to accommodate repeats, especially on the walls. However, the wallpaper designs with smaller motifs are much more forgiving and will be able to work happily around alcoves, niches, and sloping ceilings. An alternative is to restrict the pattern to the furnishings, choosing the designs to suit the dimensions of the furniture. Another way to bring interest to flat surfaces is by using texture. The chunkier the texture, the greater variety it brings, as the play of light creates shadows for an all-over patterned effect.

Inspired solutions

◆ **Scale is the key** when choosing patterns. This is especially important in small or awkward rooms, as there may not be enough space for a balanced number of complete repeats. Especially when considering wallpaper, work out just how many full repeats can fit on each wall.

◆ **Smaller motifs** are the safer option for any awkwardly shaped room. Matching designs with large repeats becomes very tricky if walls are interrupted by alcoves, niches, or sloping ceilings.

◆ **Make the motif a focus.** If you can't fit in many repeats, you could create a statement by doing the very opposite and use just one repeat. If you find a striking motif that centers perfectly onto a chimney, for example, you could make it a focal point, then pick out the colors for decorating the rest of the room.

◆ **Textures are a sophisticated alternative.** They provide relief from plain walls and complement the room without dominating it.

▶ **Pattern perfection**
The small scale of these geometric patterns means they can be teamed successfully while perfectly complementing the proportions of the room. The introduction of floral and toile de Jouy pillows adds emphasis to the color scheme. The deeply textured flooring adds further subtle interest.

◀ **Pretty clever**
This tiny room is full of interest, introduced both by pattern and by texture. The sophisticated combination turns what could be plain into undeniably pretty.

The sheer drapes are embroidered to provide subtle additional pattern at the window.

The quilting on the comforter lends classic texture to the bed, which is thrown into relief by the light coming through the window.

The large motif on the quilt might appear to go against all the scale recommendations, but it works because it relates to the size of the double bed. Three motifs fit well both across the width and down the length of the bed.

A herringbone jute carpet brings sophisticated texture to the floor, and it is both hard-wearing and soft underfoot.

WINDOW TREATMENTS

When space in rooms is limited, simple window treatments are the best policy. Elaborate curtains are best kept to rooms of generous proportions with high ceilings, which allow for a fullness of fabric and elegant drape. But simple need not mean dull. There is a wide choice from which to choose: stylish, unfussy roller shades; efficient Venetians; sophisticated Roman shades; pretty Austrians; or any drapes with simple or restrained headings. Whatever your choice, bear in mind that the window is the natural light source for the room, so choose fabrics for the window treatment that are generally paler than the rest of the room.

Inspired solutions

◆ Let in as much light as possible by keeping treatments clear of the windowpanes. This is especially important in smaller rooms with limited light.

◆ Simpler treatments, such as roller or Roman shades, work best in awkwardly shaped and small rooms. For an elegant sense of cohesion, team the fabric color with the walls.

◆ Make windows complement the room proportions. Small windows make a small room look even smaller, so visually enlarge them by using extra-long rods or cutting full-length drapes.

◆ Simple, modern panels look stunning. Choose crisp, plain fabric for a sleek look and hang from loops, ties, or curtain clips.

▶▲ Smart and crisp

A trio of crisp white Roman shades makes an ideal solution for these pretty kitchen windows, giving them a "dressed" feel without compromising the architecture.

▶ Sheer delight

With barely any need for drapes, a delicate sheer lace panel adds a feminine touch to French doors. It is the ideal solution for a small bedroom whose main charm is the natural light that floods in from the patio.

The rod is extra long so the drapes can fall well clear of the window, and the light can shine unhindered into the room.

The drapes are made from a long length of fabric that has been loosely wound along the rod and then allowed to fall on either side of the window.

Drapes, cut longer than the window, visually enlarge the whole area.

The slender drapes do not overwhelm the window, yet they are gathered enough to create an attractive arrangement of fabric.

Tiebacks add a subtle flounce to the drapes while keeping them under control on either side of the window.

Delightful rosy pink toile de Jouy has a cream background to team with the walls.

◄ **Clever combination**
These pretty drapes have been elegantly swagged to show off classic toile de Jouy fabric, yet they are restrained enough not to overwhelm the tiny window.

USING MIRRORS

Play visual tricks with mirrors both to give the appearance of expanding cramped rooms and to magnify the light, which further contributes to a feeling of space. It's not a new idea, but it works every time.

There are two routes to explore. The quickest and simplest is to buy an attractive wall mirror, which will not only perform the requisite light tricks, but will add a decorative effect to the room.

A more architectural route is to use plate mirror over a large area, or even to cover a whole wall, which has the effect of doubling the dimensions of the room. This is not a do-it-yourself option. You'll need professional glass suppliers and fitters to accurately measure the walls, then cut and fit the mirror. They understand the potential difficulties, especially in older buildings whose walls may not be true owing to movement beneath the foundations. They can make the most effective visual allowances for corners that are not perfect right angles, adjusting the mirror where necessary.

Inspired solutions

◆ **Maximize the effect by positioning a mirror** opposite a light source, such as a window or doorway. If there are times of the day or year when direct sunlight reflects in the mirror, also provide shutters or shades to reduce the dazzle.

◆ **Consider the reflections.** The effect will only be gorgeous if what you're reflecting is beautiful. However, an ugly view can be improved, for example, with a pretty sheer panel covering the window that is being reflected.

Plate mirror clads the entire end wall of this tiny bathroom, visually doubling its size.

A pretty Venetian-style mirror brings a decorative touch to the bathroom, and at the same time helps to increase the light level. Even the frame is made of mirror, accentuating the effect.

◄ The double effect

The choice of plate or framed glass needn't be an either/or option when it comes to mirrors. Both tricks have been used in this contemporary bathroom to great visual effect.

The mirror rests on the top of the tile wall border, and so doesn't interfere with the tiling detail of the floor.

◄◄ On reflection

These mirrored door panels demonstrate a clever mid-point between plate-mirrored walls and decorative framed mirrors. The panels offer a generous expanse of mirror, while the door frames are a simple decorative border.

◄ Antique charm

Part of an antique wall panel has been fitted with an elegantly decorative mirror. There is a generous reflection of the dining area adjacent to the hall, which brings light to a gloomy hallway and visually opens up the space.

FLEXIBLE FURNITURE

For effective use of limited space, seek out furniture with a split personality. Sofa beds are the classic example: sofa by day, bed by night when guests come to stay. But that's just a start. Tables can be sized for family most of the time and expanded to accommodate lots of guests when entertaining. Other tables can stand neatly folded up to one side, yet quickly jump into action with the lifting of a side leaf or two. Refectory benches might not look so flexible, but there's always plenty of potential for squeezing in—a great bonus when entertaining family and lots of little bottoms need to be accommodated.

Some furniture is designed to be flexible on an even greater scale. Loft beds, for example, take advantage of vertical space, providing a sleeping platform above an area that can be used for clothes storage, play, a spare bed, a sofa, or even desk space. It's an excellent choice for a child's room as the space under the bed can be changed and adapted to suit current needs.

Inspired solutions

◆ **Assess your lifestyle**—but if you have a family, think five years ahead. Inviting another couple over with a toddler right now might not be too challenging: in five years time, you're likely to need eight or more seats for a family lunch, so think expandable tables. If the guest room is likely to be needed by a growing child, plan for a sofa bed in the living room. Beyond the toddler stage? By the time they're halfway through elementary school, they'll be approaching the sleepover years, so think bunk beds, loft beds, and futons.

◆ **In the bedroom,** make use of space under the bed. If you don't have enough height for a loft bed, buy a mid-height captain's bed. Some have integral chests of drawers; others have space underneath for playthings.

◆ **Make desk space work** twice as hard by installing a pull-out keyboard under the worktop. That way, when you're not using the keyboard, you have the full desktop available for working.

▲ **Night and day**
While sofa beds are designed for occasional guests, here's a piece of furniture designed for nightly sleeping. But with a bench-like backrest, it can be dressed as a sofa by day. This one takes on a theatrical guise with medieval-style canopy and drapes that can be drawn for instant "tidying" in case visitors arrive unannounced.

▶ **Multiplication table**
This beautiful oak table perfectly fills the center of a summerhouse most of the time. When folded down and moved to one side, it becomes an ideal buffet table, leaving space for many guests to circulate.

The deep leaves of this gateleg table offer ultimate flexibility. It's a generous table when both leaves are up; a useful buffet table when one side is down; and a slim console table when both are down.

Slim legs are dainty and elegant, so even when fully open this table is a graceful piece of furniture.

Folding down to a narrow strip means this table is easy to move, even through narrow doorways. Ideal in this summerhouse location, where it's often moved outside for al fresco entertaining, it would be just as useful in a small apartment. It could "live" folded down as a hallway console, then moved into the living room when needed for entertainment.

OCCASIONAL FURNITURE

Where space is at a premium, look for occasional furniture that can be used for one function most of the time and pressed into action for something quite different on other occasions. For example, a generous circular table that is a side table most of the time can be moved to center stage for dining when guests are expected. Dining chairs that spend most of their time tucked into corners all around the apartment (as bedside chairs, in the bathroom, in the hall) can be gathered together around the round table whenever they are needed.

If you're really short of space, look for furniture that can be folded, stacked, and stowed away. Folding tables and chairs can be very useful as they can be tucked into a closet when not needed. Nesting tables can stand stacked under the largest for most of the time and brought out when more surfaces are needed. Think, too, about stowable furniture that might be built in, such as wardrobe beds, pullout ironing boards, and breakfast bars.

Inspired solutions

◆ **Make a display** of folding chairs by hanging them on decorative hooks on the wall, ideally near to the spot they're likely to be needed.

◆ **Use a large circle of plywood** on top of an occasional table to enlarge it, ensuring that it's not so much larger than the table underneath that it topples over. Covered with a cloth, it will be classy enough for dinner guests. When not needed, it can be neatly stowed out of the way.

▶ **Making it an occasion**
Here's a room that's hardly huge and hardly cluttered, but with guests expected for Christmas, there are seats for eight.

Evocative ethnic stools are good for occasional seating. When not needed, they're attractive enough to become part of a display.

The folding chair provides extra seating for guests. When the party's over, it can be folded and stowed elsewhere.

▲ Guest appearance

Most of the time, this room looks like most other living rooms, but when a guest is expected, the bed platform is lowered into position for a comfortable night's sleep.

Occasional tables are usually neatly nested at the end of the sofa. With guests coming, they can be brought out and placed around the room so that everyone has a place to set down his drink.

EVERYDAY DISPLAY

How you display pictures on the walls and your belongings around the home is very personal. The things you choose to have around you not only say a lot about your likes, dislikes, and motivations, they usually have powerful sentimental value, too. Most of us have photographs of our loved ones and snapshots of special or happy occasions. Many of the possessions we choose to display might remind us of holidays, trips, and friends; or they may simply be a testament to the exquisite shapes, textures, or colors that we love. Much of the art of display lies in proportion. One or two large items will create more impact than many small things, which is especially valuable in a room without much spare space. However, if you do have collections of small things you love, you can add impact by grouping them together on a shelf or in a cabinet that relates to their size. This helps prevent a cluttered look, which is not conducive to making a small room look larger.

Displays of collections look strongest if there is a link between the items. This link can be the type of items, their scale, or even their color. Displays used as a focus need to be thought of in the opposite way. They might consist of one stunning piece. Whether it's a prized sculpture or a favorite plant, if it's striking, it can be displayed on its own—on a ledge, column, or in an alcove—filling the space.

▲ All dressed up

A collection of antique Christening gowns is far too pretty to be packed away in a drawer, but hung from a peg rail on pretty white satin hangers, they can be enjoyed every day.

◄ Pretty useful

Some of the best displays make use of everyday possessions. These bags and belts haven't been hidden away. Instead, the bags are linked by type and by the peg rail on which they are hung, while the belts are given form by being coiled up and grouped as a tabletop display.

The potted orchid provides a central display and is accessorized by a candle and a book. By arranging the whole ensemble on a tray, the group is given a single identity for extra impact.

The black and white photographs on the wall have been given several links: they all have wide white mounts and the frames, are in a similar style, and all are either aluminum or beech.

▲ Great groupings

The plasma screen has been incorporated into this display of photographs, while the orchid makes up the centerpiece of a focal display on the coffee table.

Grouped closely around the plasma screen, the photographs make a stunning display.

The small tables are both in dark wood. Positioned at either side of the white chair, they add focus to the wall of photographs.

ROOM
BY ROOM

FUNCTIONAL SOLUTIONS

The function of each space makes its own demands on the effective planning of small spaces, so the basic principles need to be adapted for each room of the house. The needs of a hardworking kitchen are very different from those of a bathroom, although both are the most complicated rooms in the house, needing running water and the provision of waterproof surfaces. While a successful kitchen relies on the smooth working of several different functions (cooking, eating, washing up, entertaining) and the happy coexistence of several, if not many, people, bathing is generally a solitary affair that needs little circulation space. Bedrooms are rarely designed for more than two people; living rooms are generally more sociable spaces. All this affects priorities, furniture needs, and circulation space. These are the issues addressed over the next 82 pages to help you think through what is right for you and your lifestyle.

The efficient planning of any home depends largely on appropriate storage and never more so than in smaller spaces where a clutter-free look becomes a priority. For this reason, while the principles of storage have been tackled from page 24 onward, the particular needs for each room have been addressed in this chapter to help you make use of every stackable and stowable inch.

▶ **Movable feast**

Small rooms often mean that entertaining space has to be a part-time affair. Here, when guests are expected, a pretty wooden folded table comes out of the closet and is set up for dining with room for six.

▲ Bare essentials

Priorities arc thrown into stark reality when furnishing small spaces. A bedroom's priority is the bed plus a little hanging space for clothes, which can always be accommodated with hangers hung on large coat hooks fixed to the wall. But limited doesn't have to be unlovely. This pretty bed has been centrally positioned in front of an attractive window to create an inviting guest room out of a tiny space.

LIVING

flexible

open

light

multiuse

divisions

space

impact

simplicity

planning

lifestyle

comfort

A TIGHT FIT

Juggling the pressures of a modern lifestyle means that, more than ever, we need to be able to relax in our own private oasis at home. Invariably, nowadays that means a living room or seating area arranged around a home entertainment center. The challenge of small or awkward rooms is to find enough space to provide seating for everyone plus ample storage to neatly stow the inevitable DVDs, CDs, and videos together with books and magazines, while adding touches of flair and personal style. Excellent built-in storage that neatly accommodates entertainment disks, playstations, and joysticks can be the key to creating a sleek look that helps to give an impression of space in smaller rooms.

When it comes to seating, the successful solution may not always be the most obvious one. Received wisdom states that small rooms demand small furniture. But this is not necessarily so! Sometimes it is easier to assess the number of seats you need and then find the neatest way to fit them in, even if that's at the expense of circulation space.

The secret when it comes to a small or awkward living room is that less really *is* more, and the fewer elements you include, the more open and airy the room will appear. Decorative touches, too, are best kept simple. A few larger pieces create impact and add personality to a room without making it too cluttered.

Two large sofas facing each other provide ample seating for six while creating a streamlined look. The same length as the window, they neatly fill the space to ensure maximum seating.

▶ **Streamlined solution**

Streamlined simplicity brings an open look to a small living room. The furniture has been chosen to fit the proportions of the room, giving plenty of comfortable sitting space and all the home entertainment has been built into made-to-measure units. Uncluttered louvered shades add a fresh, open look to this modern yet relaxed living space.

Just two pictures are all that's needed to add interest to the unabashed home entertainment area.

The remaining space has been used to provide storage: cubbyholes for the telephone and fax machine plus reference books at the top; drawers down below for compact disks.

The original chimney has been cleverly adapted to incorporate all the home entertainment needs. Custom-made divisions house the television, tall speakers, and stereo system. The top section makes ideal display space.

The four carefully placed groups of accessories add personal style while remaining uncluttered.

The large coffee table—its width matching that of the fireplace opening—continues the room's simplicity.

Modern printed sofa covers have color and flair; their burnt orange tones are accentuated by the matching plain cushions.

▲ Tailored to suit

Where space is at a premium, make use of every corner. A window seat has been built into this alcove, giving plenty of seating space for two without even encroaching on the main part of the room.

FURNITURE TO SUIT

Where space is at a premium, furniture planning and buying become even more of an exacting business. There's less margin for error than in larger rooms, and you want to avoid a crowded look that will visually diminish the room. Start by drawing a scale plan, carefully measuring and recording each dimension. Mark any doors and windows, noting which way they open and begin to work out on paper what seating you might like and where.

This is the time to assess how you would like to use the room. For example, you might feel there are too many openings. Sometimes, too many doors and windows make planning comfortable seating almost impossible. Could you close off one door? Would this improve the circulation and the way in which the room is used? Don't be afraid to think big. It's better to fill one wall with a long four-seater sofa, or even two walls with a generous corner unit, than to compromise with a three-seater and single chair.

Keep all this in mind when you go shopping, carefully measured plan in hand. Take the maximum dimensions of each piece and work out how it would fit on your plan. Sitting rooms don't require too much circulation space and a few large pieces can offer more seating and create an illusion of space more readily than would the clutter of lots of small pieces.

▶ **Make a statement**

When space is limited, two large comfy chairs are all that's needed. When guests visit, the chairs can be pushed back to the edge of the room, and the bench on the back wall comes more into play. The shelves running in front of the window double-up as a display area as well as book storage.

▲▲ One plus two makes four

When space is really tight, consider using just two chairs and a generous stool. With no arms, there's plenty of room for two people to sit diagonally on the corners of the stool, easily making space for four. The choice of palest cream yields a wonderfully open feel.

▲ Taking a corner

Making a huge comeback by popular demand, corner units can offer the perfect solution in tight spaces, providing comfortable seating for up to seven people. All you need to add is a generous coffee table.

BUILT-IN STORAGE

Efficient storage eases tidying, and while living rooms may not need quite the same complexity of planning as other rooms, much of what needs storing is in bits and pieces and not necessarily gorgeous to look at. Books, CDs, videos and DVDs have a way of multiplying and are continually in danger of becoming messy. The solution is to provide as much compartmentalized storage as possible so everything can be "filed" away by type and in alphabetical order for easy retrieval.

The most efficient storage is made to measure, taking up whole walls, alcoves, or crannies, encroaching as little as possible on the main part of the room. By dividing the shelves into compartments, you not only ease the storage of different categories, but strengthen the weight-bearing capabilities of long lengths of shelving.

If you're not enchanted by the visual appearance of books and disks, store them neatly behind cupboard doors for a sleek modern look, leaving display shelving free for more decorative items.

▲ It's a cover up

Built-in units can be designed to store a variety of items by incorporating cupboards, drawers, pullout files, and shelves. The variety of door and cubbyhole shapes gives the finished unit a great deal of interest.

▲ Stealing space

With no space for freestanding shelves, the only option for this tiny room was to build display storage around the window to fill the whole wall. It's a simple idea, and when filled with fascinating decorative items, it adds character to the whole room.

◄ Wall-to-wall storage

Built-in storage does not have to be homogeneous. Most of this made-to-measure shelving has been allocated to stacking books, but right in the center is a larger compartment designed to house the television.

FREESTANDING STORAGE

Freestanding storage introduces a new furniture element into the room, often offering surfaces for decorative lighting and display, while neatly housing living room necessities. The piece is at its most efficient when it relates to the proportions of the room, possibly fitting into an alcove or running most of the length of a wall. Many modern units are divided into compartments—sometimes of different sizes—for efficient storage, and some, such as media storage, are designed to neatly accommodate modern technology.

Ready-made freestanding storage is usually a more economical option than customized made-to-measure. Yet, if carefully chosen, it can be equally efficient. Just as with built-in storage, carefully work out exactly what you need to store so you can buy a configuration that works for you and your needs. Some manufacturers produce modular self-assembly storage consisting of open-shelf units and cupboards which can be put together to suit your needs perfectly.

▶ **Classic style**
Freestanding storage doesn't have to be limited to modern homes. This elegant bookshelf, with space below for a television, works perfectly in a classic living room.

▼ **Simple style**
A modern-style sideboard provides simple storage. This piece is made up of three units positioned side by side, offering space for books and media disks and providing a surface for display.

FINISHING TOUCHES

It is the finishing touches that transform a house into a home. Without them, a room would look like little more than a furniture showroom or a model home. Collected over the years, it's the accessories and finishing touches that offer an insight into the personalities who live in the home. Paintings and photographs, found objects evoking happy holidays, a favorite lamp, or the latest interior colors represented by sumptuous cushions scattered over the sofa, bring the room alive.

Small rooms look best when they're not cluttered: conversely, a few large objects add a greater feeling of space than many small ones. If you have a collection of small items that you love, display them in a little cabinet or arrange them on a narrow shelf where they can be seen and appreciated up close.

You can also use display to transform awkward nooks and crannies into features. Try painting them in a slightly different shade than the rest of the room to set off a favorite sculpture or plant that fills the alcove.

However, the key to making the most of the finishing touches is the way in which they are arranged. Depending on the look you're after, pictures, for example, can be grouped informally for a relaxed feel, or arranged in singles, pairs, or trios for a more minimal look. Use cushions to introduce extra color to a scheme—or even to announce the change of season. Trimmed differently, they can also inject quite different personalities into the room. Neatly piped cushions, for example, lend a feel of city chic, while with tassels, they look much more Bohemian. This can be accentuated by the style of decorative lighting, sculptures, and other objects, and the way they are positioned.

Use accessories, too, to change the appearance of a room. For example, mirrors that are hung in narrow rooms can make the space appear twice as wide. They reflect the light; so all gloomy rooms benefit from mirrors, especially if they are hung opposite the window or French doors.

▶ **Dramatic display**
Bold African basketwork and wooden stools make a striking display without cluttering this small room. They have been grouped on dark wood shelves, adding stacks of personality in a simple room.

▶▶ **All together now**
When the room has limited wall space, arrange all your pictures as a group on the wall that you do have. It works here because all the frames are made in gilt with matching white mounts.

COOKING

open plan

flexibility

efficient

easy

lifestyle

family

country

sleek

clean

smooth

relaxed

MAKING A PLAN

Of all the rooms in the house, the kitchen works the hardest. No longer simply a room in which to cook, the kitchen has become just as much a living space—and can be a favorite place for the family to congregate, eat, or do homework in, even to entertain friends. More than ever, the kitchen has become the hub of the household, and no amount of time that is spent in careful planning is wasted.

Start by deciding the overall look and feel you'd like. Do you want a separate kitchen, or would you like one that incorporates eating, and even living space? Do you like everything stacked behind cupboard doors, or do you like to be able to see your most used items and to have them close at hand? Do you love the relaxed country look featuring shelves laden with pretty china, jars of ingredients, and baskets of sumptuous fresh fruit? Do you like to cook in private, and leave the after-cooking mess behind closed doors until everyone's gone home? Or do you see cooking as sociable with everyone joining in? These are all questions you need to answer before even beginning to plan your needs—especially if the amount of space you have is limited. Your answers might require planning in structural work if, say, you want to turn two smaller rooms into one large one.

Next, you need to choose the cupboard styles, floor, and wall finishes, and then plan the working area layout. Start by working out where and how you want to arrange the cooking area (see pages 76–77), and then work any living or dining spaces around it. The key to keeping the cooking area efficient, especially in small spaces, is to provide as much storage space as you can, making use of every niche, nook, or cranny, planning exactly what you want to store and where.

▶ **Classic elegance**
The flush cupboard doors of this kitchen give it a sleek, modern look. A classic galley-style kitchen, it provides a perfect work triangle, with the stove, sink, and refrigerator within easy reach of each other.

The simplicity of the decorations—plain white walls behind the wooden cupboards—visually opens up the space.

A walk-in pantry provides plenty of space for food storage as well as all those bulkier items that appear in the kitchen, such as pots, grill pans, and fish kettles.

The cork floor and moldings match the countertops and team with the wooden cupboards, ensuring an unfussy look that has a sense of space.

A section of countertop at the end of the kitchen accommodates two tall chairs, providing an ideal breakfast bar, which does not encroach on the main kitchen space.

Open shelves provide ample storage for everyday items, such as plates, bowls, ramekins, mats, and baskets for linens and cutlery. Neatly displayed, they add a decorative element to the room.

Plenty of storage allows easy cleanup after cooking so that clutter can be kept at bay.

▲ Minimal chic

A carefully planned row of cupboards and a generous island unit create ample cooking facilities in a small space at one end of a larger room used for dining and living. It has been given a personal style with elegant open shelves used to display everyday china and glass. With its clean, unembellished lines and uncluttered surfaces, this modern kitchen makes for easy maintenance, while the combination of stainless steel and pale finishes helps to visually open it up.

▲▲ Contemporary country

Molded cupboard doors give a country look to this well-planned kitchen. The kitchen area is compact with the breakfast bar providing a boundary facing onto the living area for open-plan food preparation.

THE WORK TRIANGLE

Although the kitchen is often the busiest room in the house, efficient food preparation areas can be fitted into very small and awkward spaces. Ships' galleys and restaurant kitchens are two examples of professional kitchens that are invariably tight on space. The key to efficiency is careful planning with the overall aim of creating the classic work triangle. The theory behind this is to create a triangle between the sink, refrigerator, and range, with no more than two arm lengths between them. To ensure efficient working, the triangle should not be broken by a through route, or even by a piece of furniture like a table or island unit.

You also need to plan for a short run of countertop on either side of the range and the sink to give you "put-down" and "elbow" space, with a long enough stretch between the sink and range to prepare a meal. This should not be interrupted by tall units, which are best located either at the end of the counter stretch, or along another wall. The work triangle is possible to create with most kitchen shapes.

▲ U-shape
This is a useful template for tiny kitchens and U-shaped arrangements within a larger space, as here. With the range and oven at the end of the kitchen, the sink is close to the range—an ideal arrangement as you can put used pans straight into the sink without moving a foot. A refrigerator under the breakfast bar completes the triangle.

▲ Galley
With a galley kitchen, have the range and sink on one side with the fridge opposite.

▶ Square
When there is an island unit, ensure the work triangle is on one side, or you'll end up forever walking around it.

MAJOR STORAGE

An efficient kitchen is all about well-thought-out storage. The smaller the kitchen, the more critical this is. Most modern kitchens work on a unit system, and today's designs include more size variation with rows of units no longer limited by uniformity. Some cupboards and drawers now accommodate even the bulkiest of items, such as pots and pans. Others are tall and skinny with fully fitted compartments to take small items, like condiments, herbs, and spices that you'd really like close at hand next to the stove.

These developments not only give more efficient storage, they also result in more interesting design. Once the general work triangle has been planned, consider all the available kitchen cupboards, bearing in mind what you need where. For example, you may like pots, pans, and condiments near the range and oven; cups, saucers, and mugs near the kettle; and china and glass near the dishwasher for quick cleanup.

Each lifestyle demands a different kitchen, so the more thought you put into what suits you before approaching the kitchen supplier/designer or architect, the happier you will be with the end result. Start by looking through books and magazines for ideas, pulling out images you like. Next, go to local suppliers and draw inspiration from their kitchen configurations. Back home, work out a general sketch of what would suit you best. This will help your own or the supplier's designer to work out what would be the best for you.

▶ **In proportion**
Many cupboards are designed in proportion to each other to provide flexible storage and more interesting design. Here, the narrow cupboard is one-third the width of the main group of cupboards: a classically pleasing proportion. The drawers are generous enough to accommodate bulky items, while the cupboards above house china and glass. The narrow cupboard is a perfect choice for smaller items, such as stacked jars of jams, dry foods, and cans of your favorite items.

▲ All squared up
This kitchen offers maximum storage across a limited expanse of wall. Its modular design means units of a variety of sizes are incorporated into each row of cupboards, serving every storage need from small-scale cutlery to large-scale casseroles.

◀ Divide and rule
This huge cupboard is cleverly divided for flexible storage. Most of the doors swing open, but those at eye level have lift-up doors for extra visual interest.

COOKING

SMALL STORAGE

Scale is the key to efficient storage. Although large items obviously need a big space, you have the choice of stacking smaller items on almost any size shelf or cupboard. Generally, it's much easier to find smaller items on narrower shelves—cans stacked one deep, for example, are easy to see, easy to reach. A shallow drawer next to the stove can be the perfect place to keep jars of spices one row deep with their tops labeled and arranged in alphabetical order for quick seasoning.

Another way to keep shelves manageable is to arrange items in boxes or on trays. Small baking ingredients, for example, can be kept together in an open box on a food shelf. Many modern kitchen cupboards come with a choice of fittings designed to make organizing easier. These include metal dividers, pullout trays, and boxes. Carousels help make better use of corner cupboards. Think carefully about what you really need—internal fittings are only useful if they apply to your lifestyle, and wrong fittings can become a liability.

▶▲ All contained
Ingredients decanted into jars before being stacked on shelves make for easier cupboard management and also create a decorative display behind glass.

▶ Narrow management
This narrow cupboard fits well on the end wall as it hardly overhangs the top of the counter, yet it provides excellent storage for china and glass. With shallow stacking, all is visible and easy to reach. Where space is at a premium, every inch counts. Here, the cookbooks find a home above the door!

▶▶ Storage niche
Even the most unpromising stretches of wall can be made useful if you think vertically. Here, a tiny slot between pantry and window has been put to use for china storage, while the end of the island unit is the ideal space for stacking cookbooks.

DECORATING TO BIG EFFECT

Your kitchen may be small, but that doesn't mean it has to feel claustrophobic, or that you have to feel cramped. To enhance what space you do have, keep the decorations simple and the colors pale and light reflective. Stainless steel is an ideal material for small kitchens: its shiny surface behaves like a mirror, reflecting light into the room, creating a feeling of space.

Light colors open up the room and can be used on more surfaces than just the walls—pale stone floors and countertops with pastel walls can contribute to an overall light and open atmosphere. Keep window treatments simple and sleek, too. Made-to-measure shades are an excellent, unfussy solution as they let in maximum light when they are pulled up. Solid backsplashes made from stainless steel, colored glass, or stone (all cut to fit) create a more streamlined look than traditional tiles, and enhances the space. Tiles, however, remain the classic choice: if you have a small kitchen, aim to match the grout with the tiles for a clean look that visually enlarges the space.

▲ Light and shade

By setting pure white cupboards against the palest of gray walls and matching gray baseboard, this kitchen is given a feeling of light and shade. The pale color makes the walls appear to recede, visually increasing the dimensions of the room.

◄ Shade simplicity

Where the proportions are tight, keep window treatments simple. Here, a pull-down shade ensures privacy in the kitchen, without filling the window.

▲ Let it shine

Mirror-like stainless steel used throughout this kitchen reflects the light and opens up the space. Teamed with white, it suggests a less cramped room.

EATING

relaxed

formal

friends

family

share

elegant

open plan

easy living

informal

lighting

creative

FINDING A PLACE

Dining has become something of a movable feast in recent years. There was a time when the dining room was as much an essential of the home as the living room or bedrooms. Not so now. Dining rooms still feature in some homes, but more and more, they may be part of the kitchen or living room; they may take up a part of the hall, or double up with the home office or playroom. It's not so difficult for dining to be flexible because all you essentially need is a table and chairs. If space is seriously limited, these can all be folded up and stacked away when not needed, or they can be borrowed from friends or family. If you have the space, it is useful to have storage space for china, glass, linens, cutlery, and supplies, such as candles.

Sideboards are the traditional pieces of furniture for dining storage, as they also have a serving space. But glass-fronted cupboards are another option as most dining items look good and can be stacked into attractive displays. However, if you don't have the room for storage in the dining area, all those items can be incorporated into kitchen storage, which is still a logical place, because that is where the dirty dishes will be destined anyway. Once washed, they can be quickly stacked away.

▶ **Kitchen solution**
A painted table doubles up for food preparation and dining. The china and glass are stored in kitchen cupboards.

▶▶ **Elegant eating**
This pretty dining area is incorporated into an elegant living room. All the furniture belongs in the living room and is arranged most of the time for general relaxing. When it comes to entertaining, the table is moved over toward the sofa and then side chairs arranged around it for an exquisite dining area.

The sofa doubles up as dining seating when needed, providing ample room for two.

For most of the time, the side chairs stand discreetly in corners, nooks, or crannies. When needed for dining, they are gathered in around the table.

A round table is ideal for dining as it encourages convivial conversation and can accommodate more people in a smaller area. It is also a prettier shape within the living room.

A roomy cupboard offers ample storage space for dining needs within an arm's reach of the table.

DINING ROOMS

It's surprising how little space you need for dining. Take a look around any restaurant, and you'll notice how tightly packed the tables are. The reason is that most of the time the room is being used, everyone is sitting down. However, if your dedicated dining room is on the small side, buy the furniture to fit. Allow a minimum of three feet between the fully extended table's edge and wall to allow pullback space for the chairs. Sideboards and cupboards are optional extras.

If you want to use the room for something else when not dining (a playroom, for example), buy an extendable or foldable table that can be made smaller and placed against the wall, giving more space for other activities. Traditionally, dining rooms were frequently painted in rich tones, such as deep green or burgundy red, giving a cozy, intimate ambience. However, this can be a little oppressive for smaller rooms, which are more successfully "opened up" with paler shades of the neutral or .

▶▲ Narrow winner
Even tiny rooms can take on the traditional, fully furnished look if you work with scale. In this long, thin dining room, elegant furniture takes center stage with a narrow refectory-style table, a small hall console that doubles up as a side table, and a tall slim lamp table.

▶ Borrowed space
This dining room is given a spacious feel by keeping the furniture to a minimum—just a table and six chairs, allowing plenty of circulation space around the perimeter. Adding even a narrow side table would have cluttered the simple lines and the space would have felt more cramped.

▶▶ Light fantastic
This tiny dining room looks larger than it is because of the extra light "borrowed" from the bright adjacent hall, and the large mirror also reflects light into the room. The translucent Plexiglass side table enhances the space, too.

KITCHEN DINER

With our lives becoming increasingly informal, many modern homes have a dining area incorporated into the kitchen. As well as being a great space saver, this has an added advantage in that those people preparing the meal can enjoy company while adding the finishing touches. A kitchen table can be transformed for elegant dining simply by throwing over a pretty cloth and adding a few candles and some flowers.

When dining, the focus will be on the center of the table, so you can turn the lights down low in the "hinterland" of the kitchen to keep attention away from the working element. Many kitchens incorporate a breakfast bar as a quick and informal eating area. This feature is especially popular with families as simple meals can be prepared and served all in the same place.

▶ **Breakfast bonus**

For easy kitchen eating, breakfast bars are hard to beat. This one has been incorporated on an island unit that comprises a sink, work area, and storage: all you need for quick preparation and serving without moving a foot.

▼ **Country style**

This round table is the focus of a pretty white country kitchen. It's the perfect choice of furniture for families who like to prepare food together, while providing plenty of space for eating.

LIVING-DINING AREAS

For the greatest flexibility when planning a living-and-dining room, choose dining furniture that is compatible with the living room style to give an elegant, cohesive look. In that way, when you're not dining, the pieces can be distributed through the room, which could be important if you're short of space.

Folding pieces are a useful solution if there isn't room for a permanent dining area. Gateleg tables can be folded to a narrow strip, and there's a wide choice of handsome designer folding or stacking chairs, which can be neatly stowed when not being used. Variable lighting is essential for living-room dining to create ambience and allow you to focus on different parts of the room at different times. You can do this either with groups of separately controlled recessed lights, or by using standard spotlights that can be used as direct spots, or to bounce light off adjacent walls or ceiling to create atmosphere.

◀ Statement dining

The square black lacquer table makes a focal point within the living room. It comfortably seats four, and when opened out, there's room for an even more convivial six.

▲ Modern simplicity

For most of the time, this sleek beech table is an elegant sofa table, but, when pulled out, it easily seats six for dining. The white upholstered dining chairs have been chosen because they team well with the rest of the soft furnishings and so can be positioned all around the room when not being used more formally.

AWKWARD SPACES

Anywhere you can fit a table and a couple of chairs has dining potential, so even if you don't have a room set aside for dining, you may well find you have a niche that will do nicely. Because dining is usually done sitting down, careful planning means you can turn surprisingly small spaces into comfortable and intimate eating areas. Assess your home for alcoves, "dead" hall, corridor, or spaces under the stairs, or even odd corners. You may be able to fit in a permanently set-up table and chairs, or you may decide to unfold a set specially for when you have friends around. As an alternative, consider building in corner seats, window seats, or alcove seating, which can provide a surprising amount of permanent dining space.

▲ Finding a niche

This tiny space off the kitchen efficiently provides intimate dining space for four courtesy of the made-to-measure picnic-style benches and table. Not an inch has been wasted, and, far from feeling cramped, the decorations have afforded it a cheerful, sunny feel.

▲ Friendly welcome

Although it's difficult to find space in the narrow proportions of an entryway in row houses, a corner for dining can usually be found in most square foyers. Invest in a folding hall table and then just expand it for dining. Another solution is to bring in a small table from an adjacent room for an intimate dinner for four.

▶ 'Round a corner

If you don't have space for a regular breakfast bar, see whether there's a corner where you can fit a bar table and a couple of stools. You will always need to bear circulation in mind so it might be necessary to consider hanging a breakfast bar on a hinge for folding away between meals.

SLEEPING

comfortable

intimate

soft

relaxed

unwind

fresh

pretty

easy

closets

personal

cozy

SLEEPING

SLEEP TIGHT

Most houses have a bedroom or two whose dimensions offer a challenge when it comes to fitting everything in. But bedrooms don't have to be large. Space for a bed, the smallest bedside table (two if it's a double bed), and a simple dresser are all that's really necessary. If there isn't any space for a closet, you could even substitute a hanging rail or, if it's a guest room, a hat stand or peg rail with hangers to accommodate clothing. Whatever you choose, what you may have lost in space, you can make up for with a sense of luxury.

Space shouldn't stop you from making any bedroom gorgeous. After all, this is one room where being cozy counts. You can either carry the intimate theme through by decorating in deep warm colors, possibly taking inspiration from a favorite bedspread or other textile, or you can go in the opposite direction by using paler hues for a light and airy look. Dress the bed with crisp linens, sumptuous throws, generous pillows and cushions, lay a luxurious deep pile rug on the floor, and, somehow, size won't matter.

Many older houses with rooms under the eaves have the added problem of sloping ceilings that restrict headroom. Clever positioning of a built-in closet can make this space work (see pages 102–103). If that is not applicable in your situation, start by putting the tallest piece of furniture in place, then position the bed, ensuring there's enough headroom to sit up and read.

Cream fabrics with just a hint of neutral geometric pattern help keep this potentially cramped room looking light and airy.

Drapes are an attractive and practical substitute for closet doors, making a pretty cover-up for ample hanging space behind.

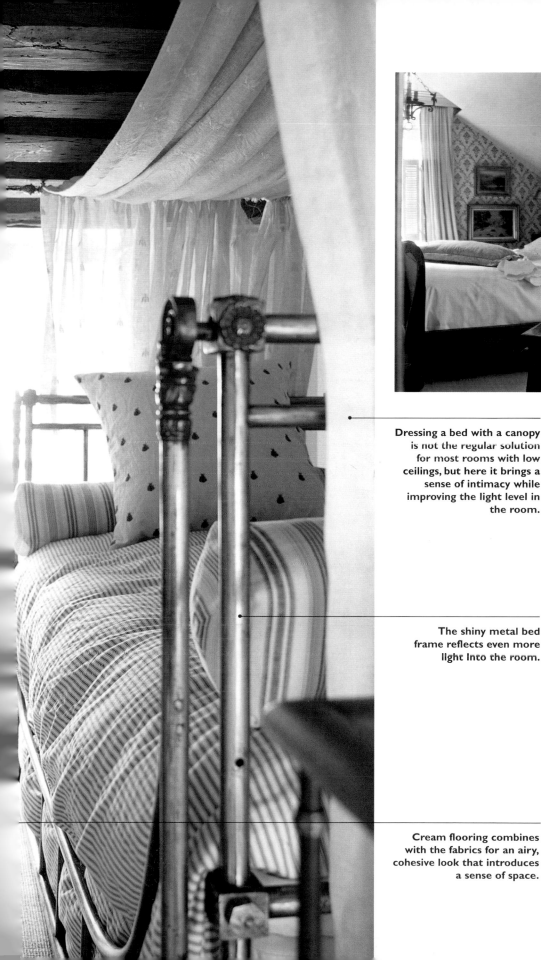

Dressing a bed with a canopy is not the regular solution for most rooms with low ceilings, but here it brings a sense of intimacy while improving the light level in the room.

The shiny metal bed frame reflects even more light into the room.

Cream flooring combines with the fabrics for an airy, cohesive look that introduces a sense of space.

▲ Making headroom

Attic rooms bring their own challenges as they dictate the positioning of the furniture. The headboard only just fits under the eaves at their lowest, which creates the impression of an intimate, permanent canopy.

◄ Silken solution

Low beams in a small room tend to look a little oppressive, but installing a false ceiling would be to deprive the room of its personality. The solution here has been to dress the room with generous swathes of light and airy silks and voiles, which transform a gloomy attic room into a more than delightful retreat.

BIG BED, SMALL ROOM

When it comes down to it, all you really need in the bedroom is a bed. If there's no space for storage, clothes can be kept elsewhere—in a closet on the landing; near the bathroom; in a custom-designed dressing room. But if the room really is going to be dominated by the bed, it's an opportunity to go overboard and make a big statement by using it to almost fill the room. With no drawers or cupboard doors to open, you won't need a lot of circulation space—just two feet on either side of the bed and two feet at the end. Measure the room and subtract at least four feet from the width and two feet from the length to give you the maximum size of bed that will fit. You could either buy an exquisite period bed, or have one designed and specially made to make the best use of the space.

▲ **Geometry lesson**
The cube of this custom-made bed fits exactly into the room, and, since it is made of the same timber, it becomes an integral part of the building. A shelf incorporated into the headboard stands in for bedside tables. The bed linens and curtains complete an imaginative solution.

▲ Light touch

Crisp white walls and simple white shades at the windows are all that is needed to set off this delightful white-painted antique metal bed dressed in a pure white quilt. These are the ingredients that combine to transform a tiny space into a pretty, light, and airy bedroom.

◄ Style statement

This striking Spanish bed, intricately carved in dark wood, adds personality to the simplest of whitewashed bedrooms. This is the best solution for strong designs such as this, which would be diminished if it were to compete with other embellished furniture.

BEDROOM STORAGE

When it comes to bedroom storage, clothes are the priority and the most efficient solution is to build in a closet. As well as the storage capacity, well-planned closets can be used to improve the proportions of awkwardly shaped rooms. For example, they can be designed to take in the slope of attic room ceilings, making use of space that would otherwise be wasted. Narrow rooms can be transformed by building closets along the length of one of the short walls, to give the room more balanced proportions.

As well as planning where the closets are to be placed, you need to think carefully about the kind of storage you need. How much of it do you want for hanging space and how much for drawer or shelf space? How are you going to store your shoes and smaller items, such as socks, ties, and underwear? How high do you want your rods positioned? Do you have many full-length garments, or are most of them short? If they're short, you may be able to fit two rods in each closet: one above the other.

Some people love the satisfaction of seeing piles of freshly laundered shirts, blouses, and T-shirts. Others prefer to hang each one individually. You might even want to have different arrangements for yourself and your children. Removing a T-shirt from the bottom of the pile without scattering the rest might be simple for you, but in most parents' experience, children and teens find it impossible.

There are plenty of manufacturers that supply bedroom closets, offering many different behind-the-doors configurations. The more you plan what you want before even visiting the suppliers, the more likely you are to end up with closets that suit your lifestyle and help you to feel so much more in control.

▲ **Pile them high**
Sweaters stacked in color-coordinated piles speed up the morning choices. The cubbyhole arrangement of the closet interior allows for just one sweater deep, making it easy to keep them under control.

◀ Divide and conquer

The key to a well-organized closet is to be able to see everything at a glance. Here, narrow shelves accommodate shoes one deep; two hanging rails hold trousers and shirts; and boxes neatly hold small items.

▲ Pretty useful

Drapes make a delightful alternative to closet doors and are a particularly useful solution where there is no space for those doors to open. This closet even contains a chest of drawers, keeping the rest of the room clutter free.

SLEEPING

ACCOMMODATING GUESTS

As guests usually stay for only a night or two, their accommodation is normally squeezed into the smallest and most awkward room of the house. Since the only real need is a comfortable place to sleep, there's little need for closets or chests of drawers, but you could provide a peg rail with several hangers, or hooks on the back of the door. You might also want to include a free-standing towel rack. Instead of a dressing table, all you need is a mirror above a mantelpiece or shelf.

For many of us, a room that is set aside for guests is a luxury, and so we have to think a little more laterally. One of the more obvious solutions is to have a sofa bed or futon in the living room, or you could put a daybed on a landing or in a lobby, and simply convert it into comfortable sleeping quarters when needed. If privacy is needed, elegant screens can be brought into play.

The other guest challenge you may meet resides in vacation homes. Here, the situation is quite different as you may want to go away with other families, which could require "dormitory" situations for the children.

▶ **The high life**
Make holiday dormitories fun for the children. Here, four bunk beds have been built into the end of a barn-like space, leaving plenty of playing space in the rest of the room. Each child has a personal space she'll enjoy even as she enters teenage years.

▼ **Landing strip**
This "dead" landing space furnished with an elegant cream daybed and armchair provides a perfect temporary bedroom. It can be screened off for a comfortable night.

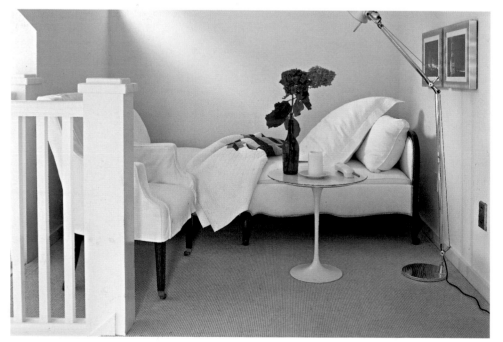

CHILDREN'S ROOMS

To successfully fit all that a child requires into even the smallest of bedrooms, plan to go upward if you possibly can. If the room has high ceilings, you could put in a loft bed, which would give a child a sleeping platform above play, desk, or even closet space. Even if sloping attic ceilings rob you of this option, all is not lost. There are many captain's beds that might not be as high as their loft cousins, but they still provide enough space underneath for storage or somewhere for a friend staying for a sleepover. Plenty of shelves are another useful strategy for awkward spaces. Even little niches can be fitted with them, while long shelves at picture-rail level make excellent homes for growing ranks of cuddly toys. Build desks into alcoves, mount bedside lights on the wall, and incorporate storage into window seats.

▲ Captain's quarters

Captains' beds allow enough space for an under-bed chest of drawers. This one has been built as a pretty module, filling all of a tiny room, yet providing all a young person would need: sleeping space, storage, and even an armchair.

▲ High and mighty

Loft beds give a sleeping platform without sacrificing floor space and can be used in any room that allows enough headroom for sitting up and reading. When calculating the sleeping height, it is important that you remember to allow for the thickness of the mattress.

◀ Perfect fit

Here, the storage has been custom made to fit around the bed. A closet has been built on either side of the bed (allowing enough space for bedside tables), and a high-level shelf between the closets makes the ideal "home" for bulky, cuddly toys.

BATHING

clean

fresh

sleek

planned

luxurious

shower

pamper

tub

concealed

smooth

white

BEST BATHROOMS

In terms of dollars per square foot, the bathroom, especially if it's a small one, is the most expensive room in the house. As well as the basic bathroom fixtures, a bathroom needs to incorporate highly engineered faucets, ceramic tiles, hidden plumbing, and possibly shower heads and glass screens, hence the high cost for the area. All these elements need to be considered when you put the plan together, but before you even begin, you need to decide on your style. There are three basic choices: the traditional Victorian look featuring freestanding clawfoot bath and pedestal basin, contemporary built-in, and ultra-modern, which consists of almost zen-like freestanding elements.

Next, decide in principle where to position the main bathroom fixtures. Aim to put the more beautiful pieces at the focal points: toilets are never lovely, so try not to make them the first thing you see as you open the bathroom door.

Even if you don't think there's a single spare square inch in your bathroom, try to eke out some kind of storage space in which to stow the endless small necessities, such as toothbrushes, toothpaste, shaving kit, medicines, and toiletries. Depending on your choice of bathroom style, this can be tackled in different ways, as addressed on the following pages.

The walls, bathtub surround, and floor have been finished in the same limestone tiles for an integrated look that gives a feeling of space.

Without the use of sliding doors, it would not have been possible to fit this bathroom next to its small adjacent bedroom.

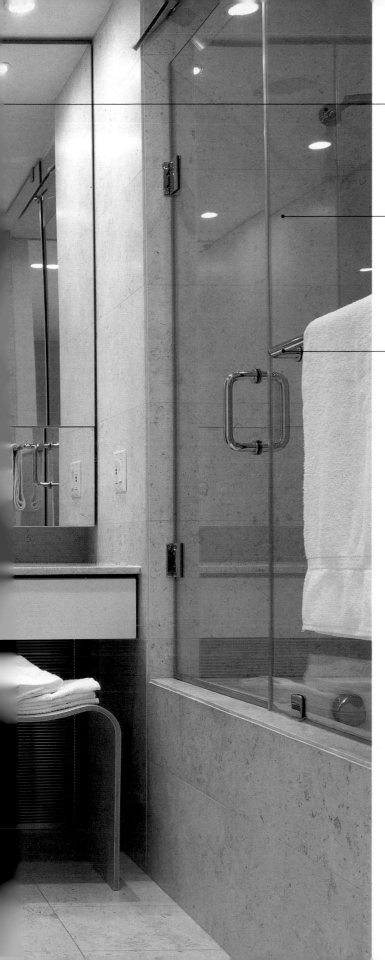

This "wall" is made up of mirror-fronted cupboards, providing plenty of storage for bathroom paraphernalia.

A full-length glass panel, reaching from bath top to ceiling, provides a watertight shower screen. The top panel can be opened to let out steam.

The chrome towel rack is a part of the shower screen—a clever solution since the lack of wall space means there is nowhere else to put it.

◄ **Tight design**

An inspired design and clever use of space have ensured this tiny slip of a bathroom includes all the bathing requirements of any modern home. The use of resilient natural materials and neutral colors means it will stay looking sharp for many years.

▼ **Simple charm**

There's nothing complicated about this pretty bathroom—a white paneled bathtub and roomy vanity unit with inset basin. The vanity unit works well with the large window, making the most of the bay.

FINDING YOUR STYLE: TRADITIONAL

A clawfoot tub is the centerpiece of a traditional Victorian bathroom, and its charm endures. There still remains a demand both for refurbished and reproduction Victorian bathroom fixtures, but traditional bathrooms are not confined to Victorian style. The classic suite comprising tub, freestanding toilet, and pedestal sink or vanity unit was popular throughout the twentieth century—and continues today—with a broad choice of styles.

Despite the convenience and generally lower cost of installation, traditional bathrooms are more "space-hungry" than contemporary built-in solutions, which make use of every inch.

◀▼ Beautiful bathing

A clawfoot bathtub is so pretty that it makes a wonderful focal point in a traditional bathroom. This one is complemented by the pretty mirror hung on the wall above. Set in a completely white room (including the floor), it combines the best of the past with a light and airy modern feel.

▼ Cool forties

Traditional bathrooms can take on many different guises. This 1940s' version features a chest of drawers that could have been used in any part of the home. It looks great and offers plenty of storage.

▲ **Basin variations**
Pedestal basins have become a perennial favorite, appearing in many different designs. This particularly generous square shape is typical of the Edwardian period.

◀ **Furnishing tricks**
The Victorians "furnished" their bathrooms in much the same way they did other rooms. Here, a dresser-like vanity unit with inset basin mimics the role of a dining room sideboard. It's a pretty piece of furniture and gives plenty of under-sink storage. The clawfoot tub is positioned in the room in a similar way to any other freestanding piece of furniture.

FINDING YOUR STYLE: CONTEMPORARY

Built-in baths and vanity units were the precursors of the fitted contemporary styale, which has become progressively more refined to make use of every square inch of space. Much of the success of these bathrooms lies in good design of the behind-the-scenes services, such as covering the plumbing and tiling and water-proofing. This not only hides these far from lovely necessities, but gives the bathroom a more streamlined look, makes it easier to keep clean, and even provides surfaces that can be used for display.

Storage is also a priority and in contemporary bathrooms most often comes in the form of a vanity unit that incorporates cupboards below the basin. More cleverly, capacious storage can be hidden behind wall panels or mirrors, providing homes for the less gorgeous bathroom paraphernalia, such as toothbrushes, shaving kits, and medicine.

A surprising amount can be fitted into a small space in cleverly designed bathrooms, and many now include twin basins and showers as well as the requisite tub and toilet. The jigsaw quality of this style is most successful when professionally designed—a service offered by many bathroom retailers who will draw up plans and work with contractors to see the job to completion.

▶▲ Slim solution
If your bathroom is narrow, back the tub and basin onto each other so the pipes can share ducting. Sliding doors are great space savers.

▶ Small but perfectly planned
Clever design ensures everything fits here without being cramped. This is partly due to the choice of a small basin, giving ample space on either side for a roomier feel.

▶▶ Bathing blues
A small space can be given over completely to bathing by tiling all surfaces—this room is one large bathing or showering experience, depending on your preference.

FINDING YOUR STYLE: MODERN

The last decade has seen an explosion of bathroom styles. Built-in has given way to freestanding style; porcelain no longer has the monopoly on basins, which are now available in glass, stainless steel, even rubber-like synthetics. Baths are available in stone and concrete composites as well as the regular enamel and acrylic, and there's been a renaissance in pedestal basin design. Bathroom fixtures have metamorphosed into freestanding designs ranging from those that are bench-like, designed to take Zen-style basins in a range of round, oval, square, and rectangular shapes, to kitchen-like units with drawers and cupboards. The success of putting them together relies even more on clever planning of the plumbing, which needs to be hidden for a successful sleek, modern, freestanding look.

▲ New dimensions

A Zen-like basin is available in a wide choice of square and rectangle proportions, which look good built onto custom-made units, like this one, or set on bench-style units in stone, metal, or wood.

▲ Freestanding bath reprise

There is a wide range of elegant modern tubs available, offering a choice beyond Victorian clawfoot. This smooth-sided design makes a stunning focal point in a modern bathroom.

◄ Benchmark

Modern bathrooms have taken on a more stylish look than in the recent past. This marble-topped bench accommodating a pair of basins is typical of the style. Even if your bathroom is small, having two basins offers a real sense of luxury.

SHOWER STALLS

If you have a small or awkward room in your house that isn't quite large enough for a bathtub, one of the most rewarding ways to use it is by installing a luxurious, oversized shower stall. Consider lining your designated area with tiles and separate the shower from the rest of the room with a glass screen. Although custom-built stalls never come cheap (by the time you've added in the cost of all the faucets, temperature controls, shower roses, and waterproofing the walls and floor with ceramic tiles or stone), if they're beautifully designed, they can bring luxury to small spaces. Alternatively, look at installing a walk-in shower, which are available complete with separate showering and drying areas—and some even offer a built-in towel rail. For yet more luxury, add a spa shower with pulsating body sprays to give an all-over body massage.

▶ **Winning solution**

An alcove running the width of this room was not long enough for a bathtub, but was ideal for a spacious shower. The addition of a state-of-the-art shower stall, incorporating both a fixed shower-head and handshower, greatly enhances the facilities of the home.

▶▶ **Finding a niche**

Built around an oval base, this shower feels roomy and luxurious, yet it takes up minimal floor space. With a fixed showerhead and a hand shower, it has various showering options. It's capacious enough to shower down two muddy youngsters at once.

WORKING

organized

sleek

efficient

light

space

storage

information

ergonomic

high tech

clean

filing

WORKING IT OUT

With computers and the Internet, the home office has become an essential space in the home. As well as a place to manage the usual household paperwork, home offices are now also used for research, shopping, and booking activities and vacations. The electronic age has meant that working from home is available to more and more people. So whereas the kitchen table used to suffice for dealing with household bills, nowadays we need room for more technology.

A home office needs to accommodate a wide range of hardware. It also needs a telephone outlet and enough sockets to supply the machinery, though the advent of wireless connections may soon reduce today's tangle of office cables. Your space might be a dedicated office (see pages 124–125) or hidden away in a corner somewhere (see pages 126–127). Wherever it is, installing one does not need to be costly. There is a wide choice of self-assembly fixtures, ranging from desks with built-in bookcases, computer housing, and keyboard shelves to various computer table combinations, all of which can be adapted to suit many different situations.

▶ Two's company
Even home offices sometimes have to accommodate more than one person. One solution is to create back-to-back workstations and use adjacent areas for storage.

▼ Smooth operator
The ultimate in minimalism, the success of this neat office is attributable to the wall panels that conceal all the familiar office paraphernalia, such as cables, storage, and office machinery. By removing it from sight, the cleared surfaces create a sense of efficiency and space.

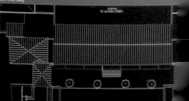

Shelves along the full length of the one dedicated office wall provide ample storage space. They have been positioned on the wall to accommodate their contents—just far enough apart so the green telephone books fit perfectly. This makes the most efficient use of space.

This office requires extensive library storage, so the shelves have been fixed in an adjacent space that is easily accessible from the workstations.

The made-to-measure drawers for blueprints provide storage for larger drawings, while their top has ample work space.

A traditional work lamp supplements overhead recessed lighting.

THE DEDICATED OFFICE

The ideal solution for the smooth running of household business is to find room for a dedicated office. All the family's paperwork, such as household bills, mortgage payments, insurance information, school reports, and tax and medical records, can be shut away out of sight in efficient storage systems for easy retrieval when needed. But home offices are no longer just about bureaucracy. Instead, in recent years, they have become much more of a family room, with the younger members of the family surfing the Internet for both homework and leisure.

A well-planned office is easy to keep neat, orderly, and under control. The best solution is to have the desk or desks against the wall for easy access to the electrical and telephone/cable outlets. Many desks have a "vanity panel" at the back, which helps to conceal the cables, thereby retaining a sleek and efficient look. If you're short of space, look for a specially designed component office. Desktops are available in square modules, half-circles, or corner units that can be put together to suit the size and proportions of available space, then supported by metal leg structures. Add to that computer housing, drawer, and filing units, and you can put together exactly what you need. The alternative is to buy an all-in-one desk with drawers, pullout keyboard and mouse shelf with bookshelves above. If you prefer a more traditional home office space, it's hard to beat the classic secretary, which neatly combines all you need with a hinged pull-down desktop, drawers, and filing compartments. The appeal is that when you stop work, you can simply shut all the clutter away behind the closed desk leaf.

▶ **All in order**

Even the decorative touches on this desk, such as the row of tiny potted plants, reflect a meticulous mind. With the advent of laptops and the move toward a paperless office, the neat desk is becoming more easily attainable.

▲ In style
Home offices often reflect the interior design of the rest of the house. Here, the traditional furniture has been teamed with simple freestanding bookshelves, providing a comfortable office environment.

◀ Dividing line
This sharp modern office has been built in a minimal area, sectioned off from a larger room by translucent sliding doors—a great space saver.

USING A CORNER

Modern technology has made it much easier to create an office in the corner of almost any room. Now that computers and other office equipment have become so much more streamlined, cleverly built-in desks and shelves can accommodate a surprising number of office needs. Invest in a sleek laptop and all-in-one printer/scanner/fax, and you'll be surprised how neat your home office space can be. If need be, nearby cupboards can always be brought into use for organizing surplus storage and filing. Almost any room in the house can offer office space, though for your own sanity, you'll want to be able to quickly put away reminders of work or household paperwork when it comes to relaxing at the end of the day.

▲ Fitting in
If space is limited, a work area can be set up at the end of any room—in this instance, a bedroom. The desk needn't be tailor-made either. Any piece of furniture that suits you from both a style and practicality perspective can be used.

▲ Shoestring chic

This supremely elegant desk has been made using simply plywood and shelving brackets. It is inexpensive but stunning, enhancing its bedroom location. The laptop provides streamlined efficiency.

◄ Smart work

This smart study plays host to an elegant office corner, courtesy of a sleek desk built in by the window. The original closet to the left of the desk provides the perfect storage for books and filing.

OFFICE STORAGE

Excellent storage has to be central to efficient working. Even as the paperless office beckons, there's still a need for filing. Household bills, mortgage and insurance documents still arrive through the mailbox, school reports and medical records need to be kept safely, and stationery and office consumables also need a home. Whether you have a separate room, a corner in a room, or even a space under the stairs, aim to provide as much storage as you can, planning it carefully to make best use of the space.

Professionals start with the dimensions of the files, books, and directories to be stored, and design to those measurements. Shelves, for example, can be built to just one inch deeper than the files they're designed to hold, and divided by extra uprights to accommodate, say, six files. Another option is to buy ready-made shelving systems. Many retailers supply flexible units that consist of unit-based cupboards, drawers, and shelves so that you can put together the configuration that perfectly suits your space and method of working.

▶▲ Neat work

This arrangement of cream drawers and cupboards is the perfect solution for an office in the corner of another room because they are built for efficiency while teaming with the décor in the rest of the room.

▶ Elegant efficiency

The whole of one wall has been set aside for office storage in this living room. The shelves have been divided to make storage as efficient as possible, while some cubicles have been used for display so that there is a more domestic feel to complement the rest of the room.

▶▶ All-in-one

This desk, which has a series of small drawers, would happily hold the smaller stationery supplies, all kept efficiently at hand. Major storage and filing are kept on nearby shelving.

CONNECTING SPACES

halls

stairs

landings

circulation

links

welcome

open

safety

light

proportion

THE BEST CONNECTIONS

The hall, landings, and stairs combine to introduce a vertical element to your home. When spaces are small or unusual, create impact by decorating throughout in the same color. This successfully unites all the odd corners, angles, and niches for an open and unified look. As connecting spaces tend to be gloomy, a priority is to allow in as much light as possible. If you're having work done on the house, look at the levels of natural light. If it's very dark in places, consider installing a skylight to make the whole area look more spacious. Natural light flooding down from the top of the house can make a surprising difference, even to the ground floor. An alternative solution is to introduce light from an adjacent room, such as from the living room to the hall or landing, by opening up the space to create an open plan. Or, with less expense, you can make a window in the internal wall or create a wall of glass bricks between an adjacent room and the hall.

Although connecting spaces tend to be narrow, it can be surprising how much use can be made of them. Small cupboards may make hardly any difference to the circulation space in the hallway, yet provide ample storage for coats and umbrellas. There is often enough spare space on landings to steal a little for closets for linen or clothes storage. If it's a simpler, more instant solution you're after, consider furnishing the landing with chests of drawers for overflow storage. For halls, it's still difficult to improve on a traditional console table, which fits snugly against a wall, providing the perfect place for mail, keys, and messages.

▶▶ Working the space
Landings may be long and slim, but with clever planning, the space can be made to work hard. By building closets down the full length of this landing, it becomes much more than a connecting space, and provides spacious storage, too.

▼ A unified whole
White painted walls and ceilings offer maximum light reflection throughout the halls and landings, while at the same time also providing a cool and elegant finish.

Discreet recessed spotlights are unobtrusive yet bathe each landing in ample light, even on the darkest nights.

Open tread stairs have an airy feel as they successfully let light through into the darker parts of the halls and landings.

Fine metal handrails complement the open tread stairway.

The landing opens out into the adjacent room, allowing light to fill the area.

Elegant flush closet doors in pale timber with simple metal doorknobs are an interesting finish and also offer ample closet space.

Darker timber flooring adds definition to each floor, providing a contrast to the white walls.

CONNECTING SPACES

KEEP IT SLIM

Few halls, stairways, and landings are roomy, so the key to furnishing them is to seek out narrow pieces that fit perfectly into confined spaces. Console tables, specially designed to be attached directly to the wall at the back, are ideal candidates. The classic antique French design, with beautifully carved legs that curve out from the tabletop, always looks elegant in a hallway and has provided inspiration for endless subsequent designs to suit changing interior fashions.

But this is not your only choice. Look for pretty chests of drawers, chairs, and coat stands, which not only look good, but can provide invaluable storage space. Or, search out dramatic accessories, such as a giant vase, stunning sculpture, or wood carving, which can be placed at the top of a flight of stairs, providing a focal point at the end of a vista.

▲ All laid out

This pretty white-painted table, set with white antique china vases and bowls, makes a delightful focal point in the hallway. More plates, hung on the wall, and a white painted chair complete the look.

◀ Classic elegance

An elaborate French-style console is an elegant focal point. Classic consoles always have flat backs to fit against the walls, but the fronts are often elaborately curved with intricately carved legs. The marble top on this one is also highly practical for the hallway as the surface won't be scratched by keys or watermarked by damp gloves.

◀◀ Console style

A half-moon console is an ideal piece of hallway furniture because it sits neatly against the wall, yet brings a curved element to what is often little more than a corridor. This one is Swedish-inspired and is complemented by the white-painted chairs on either side. In this hallway, even the radiator cover is put to use as a handy hallway shelf.

CONNECTING SPACES

STORAGE

Just because they're invariably narrow, it does not mean that halls and landings have to be useless spaces. Given thought and planning, they can offer a surprising amount of storage space. What they may lack in width, they often make up for in length, which all adds up in terms of square footage. To put it into perspective, compare narrow halls and landings to a boat, where a great deal of storage space is made available in lockers along the length of the vessel—and that is without the height of a normal house.

A row of closets along the length of the hall or landing can provide ample storage. Their depth would depend on the width of the corridor, but even the narrowest could be used for shoes, as a broom closet, or for storing lightbulbs, pillows, rolled-up spare comforters, bathroom requisites, cleaning materials, and toilet paper. If you have enough space for the closets to be 14 inches deep, you could use them for office filing, while 20 inches will give you wardrobe hanging space.

When planning, make sure there is enough clearance space for doors to swing open, remembering that the narrower the doors, the less clearance space they need. If your space is very constricted, choose sleek sliding doors with recessed handles.

Full closets aren't the only option: bookshelves can be as little as ten inches deep, yet lining the hall and landing walls with them can offer copious library space. Imaginatively divided into cubicles and cubbyholes, shelves can look highly decorative, especially if the books are arranged by size or in color groups and some of the cubbyholes are given over to some of your favorite decorative items.

If you want an instant storage solution in the connecting spaces of your home, simply install a pretty chest of drawers as a linen store, for example, or to provide overflow storage for a smaller bedroom. As well as providing extra space, it will also give a more furnished feel to the area and provide a surface for a beautiful lamp or a favorite vase for flowers.

◄ Landing library

Walls lined with bookshelves can provide ample space for storing a library, especially if it extends over "dead" space, such as above the door. It's a handy trick, especially in households where the book population seems to continually grow

◄◄ Hallway store

An attractive chest of drawers makes a pretty furnishing for the hall, offering a useful surface as well as handy storage space right near the door.

◄ Wall-to-wall closets

A landing is the perfect place for adding copious storage. The bookshelves in the adjacent area are divided into rectangular sections that "jigsaw" together to make an interesting design. Interspersed with treasured objects, this wall of bookshelves becomes a highly visual element within the space.

CREATING EXTRA ROOMS

By indulging in a little begging, borrowing, or stealing, clever designers can transform small pieces of unused space into useful areas, or even into extra rooms. If you can afford to steal 27 inches off the width of any connecting space, you have space for a row of kitchen units; a similar space could offer you bookshelves that incorporate a built-in desk, but you'd then need to have some chair pullback space available in an adjacent area.

You could steal a little bit from a generous hallway to put up a table and give yourself a dining area. If you're thinking of remodeling parts of the house, you could give yourself another bathroom by combining a bit of landing with borrowed space from an adjacent bedroom of generous proportions. If the area is very small, then resort to sliding doors that don't encroach on the landing when open. Other ideas could include utilizing a little landing or under-stair space to create a powder room; or making a generous landing closet with sliding doors, which could conceal a stacked washing machine and dryer.

▲ Way-out eating

The circulation space between the bottom of these stairs and the back garden allows enough space for a farmhouse style table with seating for four, turning dead space into a comfortable dining area.

◀ Work it out

Flexible built-in shelving designed to incorporate a desk can provide an efficient work space on the landing. This works especially well if it's open to the living area, so that a little space can be borrowed to allow pullback for the office chair.

◀◀ Corridor kitchen

If the landing's wide enough, you could coax enough space out of it for an efficient kitchen. A single line of units is a surprisingly practical cooking space, and by thinking vertically and installing wall units, you'll have plenty of storage space (see also pages 78–81).